Beauty

Beyond

the

Brush

Discovering Your True Identity

K R Y S T L E   W I L L I A M S

ISBN 978-1-0980-5321-5 (paperback)
ISBN 978-1-0980-5322-2 (digital)

Christian Faith Publishing, Inc.
832 Park Avenue
Meadville, PA 16335
www.christianfaithpublishing.com

Printed in the United States of America

Introduction

An ongoing lesson for me has been understanding that my beauty and identity extends beyond my capabilities, my outward appearance, family situations, relationships, the titles and positions I've held, degrees earned, or material possessions obtained. In fact, the journey of completely understanding who I am, both physically and spiritually, has yielded some amazing revelations of what it means to authentically love and honor myself, and in doing so, I have come to recognize the magnificence of being one of God's most beautiful creations.

During this journey, I have shed many tears, overcome lots of challenges, broken down barriers, and accepted new realities and hard truths about life and myself. This process felt like an imprisoning veil had been lifted from my mind and spirit, allowing me to shift into an awareness that liberated my soul. I have exchanged negative behavior patterns for new empowering ways to live life in a manner that adds value to who I am. My focus is geared toward things that keep me balanced and aligned with peace and love. I spend more time engaging in activities that keep me grounded and bring joy to my life, such as meditating, taking piano lessons, painting, singing, and spending time with my children. Most of all, I have learned to spend time with myself, which has given me the greatest joy. My personal transformation is the result of a constant desire to become more like the divine, and during this process, I have learned to experience life in a more loving, meaningful, and purposeful way.

I now live life, as I would consider it to be, in a more excellent way. The key to it all is living life from the inside. It's about finding that place of surrender in your heart that leads you along the path of becoming more. I now understand what it means to follow my heart as I am guided by love's wisdom and grace. This journey has definitely been a gift from God. I am an extension of the creator, and he has given me the ability to demonstrate his expression through my life by me showing up in the world as I am. As he is, so am I. This is how I see myself; everything that God is I am. His essence illuminates my true nature. Therefore, he is the essence of who I am. He has made me even more beautiful than a rose and more illustrious than the sea. The beauty he gives can never be painted on or removed. It is embedded into the deep fibers of my inner being. It is my DNA.

What a remarkable discovery…to know and see myself as I really am, a phenomenal woman who has so much to offer the world. I hope that you will begin to see yourself in the same light, as a phenomenal woman who has a lot to offer the world.

My prayer is that you are willing to surrender yourself to a similar journey of discovery. No matter how challenging the roads are up ahead, make a commitment to yourself that you will not give up. Be honest enough with yourself to walk in the path of what you have discovered to be true about who you are and the reality of your current circumstances. The choice of how to move forward with what you discover is up to you. Nonetheless, acknowledgement and acceptance of your reality, whether it is based on facts or fantasies is the first step to healing. Be strong and courageous enough to experience the possibility of pain and discomfort that may accompany what you discover. It's okay to experience uncomfortable emotions. This is normal. However, it is not okay to ignore your emotions as if what you are feeling is unreal. Negative emotions are uncomfortable and typically an indication that what is going on inside of us requires attention. We must be willing to deal with the areas of our inner self that are wounded, to become more of our authentic self. Use your feelings and emotions as guides to help you get on the right path to living a whole and free life. If you learn to trust and follow your heart, you can rest in knowing that it will guide you along the right path. Trust me, the reward of freedom is far greater than any uncomfortable space you may experience during this process. Living a life that honors what is true in your heart leads to a life of freedom. However, we must be willing to uncover what may be hidden in our hearts in order to experience the freedom we desire.

I also pray that you are bold and fearless enough to embark on this journey of discovering your true identity…your true beauty that extends beyond anything you have ever imagined about yourself. This thirty-one-day devotional offers intuitive revelations that I gained throughout my journey of discovering my true identity. I have titled each revelation "Beauty Lesson." I believe these lessons were wisdom principles placed in my heart as God purified my soul and renewed my spirit. I hope you experience a similar transformation as you spend time reflecting and meditating on each lesson. God's anointing can transform any situation, so be encouraged as you make the decision to do the work that is required for becoming a more beautiful woman from the inside out. I pray blessings of peace and prosperity over you, and I am *super excited* that you have decided to begin your journey of living life more beautifully from within!

Beauty Lesson 1

Be Still Today

L ife can be noisy and filled with so many distractions. You owe it to yourself to practice the art of being still and quieting the noise, even if it's just for a moment. Quiet your heart and mind by removing all internal commotion. *Be still* and allow your mind and body to experience the calmness of this moment. Be still and wait. Wait for *peace*, wait for answers, and wait for the presence of God to permeate your entire being. The more you become aware of the presence of God on the inside of you, the more you will experience peace that will quiet all noise and remove every distraction. Everything begins from within.

Beauty Lesson 2
Embrace Peace Today

When life situations are overwhelming, surrendering every-thing to God brings peace to my mind and spirit. In the very moment of my despair, I relinquish it all. My feelings and emotions, every challenge, all my anxieties, pains, fears, and even troubled relationships are released. Surrendering is a form of let-ting go. As I empty out my troubled heart, the most Holy Spirit fills it with peace.

Beauty Lesson 3
Be Happy Today

Happiness shows up when I am thankful for all that I am and all that I have. It is experienced most when my soul is aligned with the Divine Spirit of love. It is my right to be happy and my responsibility to create my own happiness.

The key to being happy is recognizing the beautiful moments where God's grace has been manifested in our lives and expecting happiness to bloom as we live each day on purpose so our lives have meaning.

Find Your Inner Strength

I know for sure that God is always with me. I have the grace and support needed to accomplish every good thing. My source of strength is knowing that all things are orchestrated for my highest good. When I feel the most vulnerable, God shows me in many ways how I am strong enough to endure.

Beauty Lesson 5

Be Steadfast About Pursuing Your Goals

Whenever I take my focus away from God, I inadvertently lengthen the process and extend the time it takes to achieve my goals. There are countless distractions that can cause me to lose sight of God's plan for my life. For this matter, I shall remain focused, looking to God for guidance moment by moment. "No weapon formed against me shall prosper" (Isaiah 54:17)! No weapon formed shall steal my vision.

See Yourself as You Really Are

Allow yourself to grow into a space of inherently knowing your self-worth. Know and understand that our possibilities are limitless and that greatness has been given as a gift to anyone who will embrace it.

Hold in your heart, the notion of being one of God's most treasured creations, beautifully and wonderfully made, hand-crafted and uniquely sculpted for a specific purpose. You were created by the Greatest Being of all—one who is all powerful, gracious, and loving. This truth should nullify any doubts about the greatness that lies within each one of us. Greatness begets greatness, and excellence can only produce something that is astonishingly excellent itself. Therefore, it is imperative that we are awakened to the truth about who we are. The truth is we are both great and excellent, imperfectly perfect expressions of everything we were intended to be.

There is no need to continue wrestling with a distorted self-perception. See yourself according to your own sight. Give yourself permission to become liberated from the strongholds of misbeliefs that have inhibited your ability to take positive actions that will facilitate self-love and healing. Charge yourself with the responsibility of recognizing who you are as an extension of all that is good and excellent, the highest level of greatness. You are a child of God.

Beauty Lesson 7

Have a Clear Vision of How Change Occurs

I have the ability to change myself. That's as far as it goes. If I want my life to look different, then I must change. This simply means that I must replace old limiting mind-sets with productive thoughts and exchange old habits with new habits that promote life, joy, peace, and wellness. Change begins with me. When I redefine myself, I am redefining my life. Perhaps by doing this, I may inspire others to do the same.

Beauty Lesson 8

Be Content

Everything will be okay when you are okay with everything. Understand that what is showing up in your life is happening according to a divine plan. Contentment is not devoid of fears, anger, insecurities, or uncertainty. However, a state of contentment allows you to acknowledge what is presently happening, yet still having the courage to work through your experience while expressing gratitude for the things that are adding beauty to your life.

Beauty Lesson 9

Stand Strong Alone

There are moments in life when you must lay aside every weight in order to walk freely in your true identity.

The Spirit of the Lord said to me, "You are holding on to people and relationships that should not be. Let them go... Let these things go. I have equipped you! Be alone and yet still satisfied."

In that instance, I could clearly see that God had already placed within me everything I needed to be whole and complete. I was finally free to let go of the baggage that was preventing me from standing strong on my own.

Beauty Lesson 10

Be Open to Receive

I remember repeatedly confessing to God, "I know there is something greater on the inside of me." As often as I rehearsed that prayer, I continued to feel empty inside. Something was still missing from my life, and I couldn't identify it. I spent several years praying and searching. I read numerous books and studied countless teachings from enlightened and spiritual leaders. I even found myself generously giving to others sometimes giving too much of myself away, which left me physically, mentally and emotionally depleted. Needless to say, the void remained and my soul was still starving for more. I remember feeling hopeless, as if my life would never be complete. And then the answer came!

"Receive! Receive all that I have for you. I love you, and it's time for you to know that. It's time for you to experience my love in its entirety. Experiencing the fullness of my love will enable you to stand strong and live with boldness. Receive my love." This message from God was life changing. Seeds of hope had been planted in the fallow ground of my heart, and over time the reassuring words of his message fertilized what had been growing in the recesses of my heart all along.

I pray that you would also receive God's love in a way that will transform your life. Ask the Spirit to teach you how to experience life on a deeper level so that you can walk in the fullness of all God has for you.

Beauty Lesson 11

Make Your Life More Beautiful

B e thankful for what you have. Learn how to add color to the gray areas of your life. Instead of complaining, discover ways to bring about beautiful change to your personal universe that exists within your soul. Create a space in your life for beauty.

Search for ways to add value to your life, such as developing practices that will help you grow spiritually or discovering your inner passions that will guide you closer to your purpose.

Be Intentional About Discovering Your Purpose

L et go of everything that does not support your vision and life's purpose. To make it in this world, you must remain focused, staying single-minded on your goals. This can be achieved by having a clear understanding of who God created you to be. Only then will you begin to understand your life's work. Understanding our authentic selves always precedes what we are to do with our lives. If you do not possess full knowledge of your life's work, continue to search for it and soon enough, it shall be revealed. Whatever you seek, shall be found.

Nonetheless, keep moving forward. Finish what you begin. Be confident and persistent and wait patiently for the manifestation of the fruit of your labor. What you desire to receive is already yours, and it shall manifest. Master the art of being. Do the work of discovering. Live out your purpose.

Beauty Lesson 13

Everything Begins with Me

I must be in right relationship with myself in order to be in a healthy and productive relationship with others. I must see my true self in order to see the trueness in others. What I desire to see manifested in my external world has to first be planted and blossomed within myself.

I must have love and compassion for myself in order to have love and compassion toward others. I must give to myself and then I can freely give to others.

Draw a Line in the Sand

When you become exhausted from going through the same frustrations, hurts, and pains to the point of despair, find the strength and courage within yourself to draw a line in the sand. Tell yourself, "Enough is enough" and then follow through with sure determination that you will not turn back.

Beauty Lesson 15

Choose Well

Our life's journey is shaped by the choices we make, what we believe about ourselves, and our response to the world we live in. Make decisions based on the knowledge of knowing that you are connected to a divine source that will enable you to reach your full potential if you choose to do so.

If you feel underserving of the best that life has to offer, that life is hard and unfair, and that everyone is against you, this is the reality you will create for yourself. Our lives will always be shaped by our thoughts and how we respond to what life presents. We can either choose a life full of possibility or one that is lacking. Choose a life of limitless possibilities.

Beauty Lesson 16

Trust Your Heart

M ake up your mind to never have another discussion about why something cannot be done. Be brave enough to begin working toward the desires of your heart, and courageous enough to follow where the heart leads. Be open to receive what is presented and trust that you are supported.

Brave Surrender

B rave surrender is trusting the process of life. It is knowing that there is a higher plan beyond what you can see and sometimes understand. It is saying yes to life, yes to yourself, and knowing that everything will be okay. God will send you holy help once you decide to take the first step.

Beauty Lesson 18
Shine Your Light

As I seek the Spirit to find love, joy, peace, and strength, I find it within myself. There is no separation between me and the Spirit. I discovered that everything I have ever needed has been inside of me all along. So now I feel free to shine my light without hesitation. I will shine as a peacemaker who spreads love and joy throughout the world.

I will shine as a wonderful human being and creative bright star. I will shine as a courageous woman, a magnificent wonder. I will shine my light at full capacity as an expression of God.

Beauty Lesson 19

Create New Patterns

Reprogram your mind to think progressive, productive, and life-giving thoughts. Eliminate the pattern of revisiting thoughts of situations and people that remind you of past hurts and failures. When the thoughts arise, be a witness of those experiences without yielding to any negative emotional attachments. Stay in alignment with thoughts that make you feel good and happy. Be thankful for the opportunity to create new patterns. Move on toward forward thinking; up there, you will find love, joy, and peace.

Beauty Lesson 20
Be Willing to Move Forward

No one has ever been able to go in opposite directions at the same time. You are either going forward or moving backward. Be open to acknowledging what is holding you back and be willing to do the necessary work to evolve.

Design and Create the Life You Want

I am filled with creativity, and I will cocreate what I desire my life to be, painting my life's canvas as I see it. My creativity drives my passions and my passions develop into purpose.

When I create a beautiful world within myself, I create a more beautiful world for others.

Beauty Lesson 22

Take Your Place

I can never lose my place in God. Therefore, it is not necessary to compete with others or become fearful of being outperformed. I am who I am to God and that will always remain the same. God's love eliminates my insecurities and builds my confidence so that I may take my respective place in the world.

Accept Yourself as You Are

When you accept yourself for who you are, you will never have to worry about trying to become someone else. Be your own kind of beautiful.

Beauty Lesson 24

Develop a New Perspective

Victims view situations as always happening to them; they take things personally. A warrior views challenging circumstances as opportunities for advancement. There is a new way and a new perspective that can be developed.

This perspective is recognizing your own divinity. Understanding that every problem has a solution and everything you need shall be provided. Just as the birds have the expanse of the sky to fly, so will you have all that you need according to the nature of who God created you to be. Our limitations should only be perceived as lessons that allow us to utilize our divinity to meet every challenge with assurance that all things are possible and there are truly no impossibilities. Recognize your internal divinity. Feel it and become one with Spirit.

Beauty Lesson 25

Always Remain Hopeful

H ope is knowing that God still has a plan for me even when I can't see where I'm headed.

Be Present in Every Moment

Experiencing life on the inside is turning inward and being present during every moment with yourself and with God. It is the awareness of your thoughts, feelings, actions, and also the awareness of what is happening around you. Being present is choosing a response to your internal and external world that reflects love and peace toward yourself and others.

It is making a conscious decision to remain in that space between the past and future. It is acknowledging what is happening now.

Be Thankful during Transition

During seasons of transition, choose to be thankful for all that is good instead of focusing on what appears to be wrong. Be conscious of and live in the present moment. Press through hard times. Choose to be happy in spite of pain…in spite of fear…in spite of suffering. In the absence of not knowing what to do, seek wisdom and vision. For this season is only here for a moment, and it will soon pass away. No matter the transition, you are more than able to endure because you are equipped with everything it takes to make it through to the other side.

Beauty Lesson 28
Trust the Process

M y steps are ordered. Every encounter I experience, whether with myself or with others, is divinely orchestrated for the evolution of my soul and my life progression. Obstacles that challenge my thinking can also be viewed as opportunities to face my fears. I know that God will always have my back. Therefore, when I trust God and lean into his love, he totally supports me. I am sure to receive all that I need and desire, and I will definitely experience the manifestation of everything I expect to see happen and more.

While trusting the process, I must also do the work required. I can be certain that God is supporting my success as I do what is necessary to combine action with my faith.

Beauty Lesson 29

Find Your Place in the World

Find your place in the world by discovering your true self and passions and understanding your purpose. We must pave our own way, and if we are truly following our hearts, the path will most likely lead us to uncharted territory where we will have to decide for ourselves if we have what it takes to make this happen. The answer is a resounding yes! Yes, we have what it takes. And yes, there is a place in the world for each of us to show up as the best version of ourselves.

Be Thankful for You

God has blessed me with the gift of myself. I will cherish myself. Love myself. Be patient and compassionate with myself and thank God for giving me to myself!

Beauty Lesson 31
Show Up to Class

L ife is our universal classroom, and we must be willing to show up for our assignments. The moment we make a request to God, he begins orchestrating the necessary situations and people required to manifest what we have asked for. The Spirit guides and equips us. We must do the work of discovering, awakening and becoming the best version of ourselves.

About the Author

Krystle Williams is a nurse, educator, author, and speaker. She was born in Birmingham, Alabama, but raised in Detroit, Michigan. She graduated from the University of Detroit Mercy and the University of Phoenix and holds a bachelor's and master's degree in nursing. Krystle has used her nursing platform to serve women and children. She has devoted many years to mentoring, coaching, and supporting women, while offering them lasting hope. She is passionate about helping women overcome mental and spiritual blocks that prevent them from living the beautiful life God has ordained for them.

In her efforts to help others, she realized that she too had been on the same journey of discovery and becoming an authentic version of her true self. During her journey, she became aware of the fact that our true identity extends beyond how we physically see ourselves, the pictures we paint, and the labels we use to describe who we are. She also discovered that her vocational calling to be a nurse was for the divine purpose of loving others, spreading joy, and offering hope and healing. Krystle's devotional writing is helping women discover the beauty in knowing their true identity. She has three beautiful children and continues to seek God's wisdom in spreading love and truth to all who are open to receive.

CPSIA information can be obtained
at www.ICGtesting.com
Printed in the USA
LVHW042240310820
664669LV00002B/297